Introduction

This book is written from the premise of having a lifetime of care. From the time of my birth until the age of thirty-seven, I was cared for by loving parents. From thirty–seven, I had care from my husband until he became sick with Parkinson's disease and we needed long-term live-in care, made worse once he had to reside in a care home and I was left to the mercy of so-called professional carers, both good and bad, trying to help me survive in this very difficult, unequal world.

In the film 'The Lady in the Van' based on the account of Alan Bennett in his book 'Writing Home,' Alan Bennett states that shitting is at the forefront of care; in my opinion he has never made a truer statement.

So often, carers feel that there is no need to make the client feel valued, giving them self-worth, and self-actualisation. By the same token, carers may also feel that they have not had the best opportunities for self-development – the old adage: if you can't find a job, become a carer, just compounds the attitude that anything will do just so long as one puts a 'body' to a 'body' without looking at the needs of the person or consequences of the action - in which case, circumstances will never change. What we have to remember is that each human being, regardless of their mental or physical status, is an individual in their own right and must be treated as such. See the person and not just the problem.

My Mother used to say 'when you have a disabled child, you are as disabled as they are because you can only go at their speed'; disability and the handling of it require a great deal of patience. Most carers in my experience do not have this; those that do are a breed apart from the rest and are exceptional. Those exceptional ones are hard to find, they are like gold dust, and are worth treating as such.

The Burden of Care

The one area of guilt that I have carried all my life is the way in which my personal physical circumstances have affected the lives of so many.

In the early years, my parents, who also had two able-bodied boys, tried to do what they could to bring all three of us up in an environment that was as normal as possible, whatever that might mean; for in my house there was no such thing as normal, one never knew from minute to minute how so-called 'normal' daily life would be thrown into chaos.

My father never had any patience, he saw all the weekly drudgery of physiotherapy and trips to hospitals as yet more inconvenience to him. This burden was mostly carried by my mother who took me from our home in Poplar in the East End of London, to Hampstead three times a week by hospital transport, to the Bobath Centre. This was a specialised centre for the treatment of Cerebral Palsy.

I started my life of physiotherapy at the age of eighteen-months with a young physiotherapist called Nancy R Finnie. She was offered a chance to train at the Bobath Centre and subsequently work for them. I was incredibly fortunate that she offered me the chance to be one of her role-model patients and come with her to the Bobath Treatment Centre. I was incredibly lucky because the whole approach meant that I would have a far different structure to my general life. To the Bobath Centre, treatment was not just for half an hour, three times a week; it was indeed a whole way of life. This regime had to be religiously followed day after day, looking at every situation of posture, eating, socialisation, and every aspect of daily life. If you took your child to the Bobath Centre you had to agree to work relentlessly to try and create change.

I attended the Bobath Centre from the age of four to the age of twenty-seven, a twenty-three-year commitment; a commitment that sacrificed so much in terms of the time that my mother could give to other members of the family. For example, when one attended the Bobath centre, the level of commitment had to be all-embracing on the part of parents and family members. Two-and-a-half hours a day was the norm and it took no account of other commitments. It goes without saying, that this level of commitment was not always understood by certain members of the family, namely, my father and my oldest brother, who deeply resented the attention that was lavished upon me. It is very hard when you are struggling with all aspects of disability and indeed daily life, to realise that others have needs too, that are not just centred on you. I think so often, particularly in later years, how my disabilities must have affected my parents' marriage. There were always incredible arguments and tension. My father was one of the Old School, who believed that his wife should be there whenever he came home from work, and that she should be compliant to his needs, whatever that might mean and whenever he felt the need. She was often too physically exhausted to care as she was chasing me backwards and forwards to hospital, doing the treatment, running the home with three children, born within two years and eight months of one another, and, trying to fulfil the wishes of my father. I sat back, watching and listening, taking it all in, feeling guilty, knowing that my mother was under a great deal of pressure both physically and emotionally and I was powerless to do anything about it. My father was an out and out bully who felt he could get what he wanted by making the most noise, shouting, slamming and banging when his meal wasn't ready on time. I have known my mother to cook a meat pie on gas mark 10 within twenty-minutes of getting in from hospital to avoid a family feud.

If a week had less than three major rows in it, it was a good week. As I grew up, I frequently asked my mother why she stayed with this man, her answer was 'what do you expect me to do when I have a disabled child, I can't leave him because of you', which made me feel even more guilty. My disability was forcing her to stay when the pressure must have been intolerable. Then my mother also had criticism from my elder brother, he had some health issues of his own such as deafness and a need for emergency surgery as a twelve-year-old (he ruptured his spleen) which left him weak and unable to play sports at school for a long time. School sports days and other events were very difficult; mum could not attend them because she was dealing with my hospital treatment, and this made the boys, and particularly John, angry and resentful and left me feeling guilty. Again my situation affected the people I loved through no fault of my own (that feeling is still with me more than seventy-years later, when my situation has to affect the lives of those caring for me).

My father always carried a burden of guilt about having a disabled child because he had disability within his own family. He had a brother with Cerebral Palsy (much worse than me, his mental ability and speech were affected). Unlike myself, my father's brother was put into a care home at the age of six so that it did not affect the day to day running of his family. This event made a big impression on my father because when I was born with Cerebral Palsy, my father's reaction was that I would never be put into a home. Laudable, yes, but it wasn't dad who was carrying the real responsibility of it all, it was my mother who was worn out by the whole process. I frequently saw her cry with fatigue and frustration, and that made me feel even more guilty.

Guilt and stress were the overriding memories of my childhood, but I suppose it would be ok because I was told I would not live beyond twenty-one, but here I am over seventy years later still going reasonably strong. When one sees the dedication and the sacrifices that people make on your behalf, you are left with a feeling of total commitment to them. My mum was the main-stay of my world, she could do no wrong, and I was totally devoted to her.

The Pressure of Caring

More and more, people caring for their loved-ones go deeper into themselves. Their social life is virtually nonexistent, the consequence of this is that you are the person that they have built their life around, and the price that I had to pay was that my mum demanded total unwavering loyalty from me. She could do no wrong, and this created tension between my mother, father and myself because I constantly found that I was taking sides, even though I didn't wish to get caught up in those moments of jealousy and difficulty.

All through my life, I was reminded of the sacrifices that my mother had to make for me, in return I had to adopt the attitude that what she said, went. This is the kind of experience within any family to a greater or lesser degree, but if a parent cannot love and let go, and that love becomes total obsession, then it is abnormal and stultifying. In the end, so often, the person with disability is not allowed to think for themselves, or make a decision unless it is on the advice of the parent; in this case, my mother. If I did not comply with her wishes then woe betide me. So often, I was not allowed to make decisions even though I was totally capable and well able to decide what I wanted to do. One had to be at my mother's beck and call in the same way that she was for me. The only difference was the level of emotional blackmail that gave every decision that she did not approve of, that extra twist. "After all I have done for you" was a frequent cry. Quite frankly, I was never allowed to forget all that 'she had done for me.' I know the sacrifices were tremendous but to be constantly reminded of the fact that I 'should' be grateful, was a burden beyond belief. I felt like screaming and frequently did when no one was around. I would have done anything to 'escape.' I am now only free to express my feelings because both my parents have died. It isn't that I am trying to sully the memory of my parents but I do feel that my feelings in all of this were never understood. I had to take what I was given, and be grateful. My brothers had so much freedom in comparison to me although I am sure that they felt suffocated by the words 'ought' and 'should' and 'if only.' I longed for freedom but it was many years until it came.

It was very difficult for me making friends, because children found it difficult to play with someone who could not move or do things at the same pace as they could. So often when I thought I had found a friend and got confident in putting my trust in them, they left for pastures new. Over and over again I was hurt by this experience. This lack of confidence in myself has stayed with me to this day, and I believe has affected me quite badly within the context of the client and carer relationship.

All the time I was taught by my mother to give my best in love and friendship to the people I got close to, but often the kindness that you had shown them was thrown back in your face for one reason or another. This has happened time and time again within the role of client-carer relationships.

I always believe that if you give your very best to another human being, you make them feel wanted, loved, and valued; that is what true friendship and love is all about. The key word is respect. Sadly, respect is often lacking when it comes to associating with people with a disability. There are many people in society who do not respect you because they feel, as a disabled person, you have no valid contributions to make. We ought to be more enlightened in the so-called modern society but sadly, barriers are put up which are incredibly hard to break down. As a child, my mother would frequently say 'don't bother with making friends, you just stick to your mum'. In this remark, there was safety because I knew that she would not let any harm come to me, yet it was more pressure to make me more dedicated to her, and build my life around her sole devotion to me.

This may be safe! But it is not healthy. A person with disability needs to have the opportunity of risk -taking within their limitations, trying to stretch themselves to become a well-rounded human being.

I know in some cases, however hard you try, there will be some people whose disability is so extreme and profound, that however one tries in this regard, it cannot happen. All I am saying here is that where the person with disability has the mental ability and the intellectual freedom of expression, it should be fully exercised. Maybe we cannot go on a sports field, or a cross-country run, or anything that demands great physical activities (paralympians excluded) yet we should be helped to find our own particular level and interest, that with help we can pursue. In my case it is classical music, theatre, and aspects of the arts in general. All of which I find gives me great stimulation of the mind and great easement of a very painful body; music reaches the parts that others cannot reach.

There were times when my mother took it in her own hands to decide who I should be friendly with, and who not. She was going to particular people who I was making friends with and saying 'don't bother about Lin, go out and make your own friends, she will only hold you back'. When I tried to telephone this particular person, I was told by my mother not to push myself on to her 'she doesn't really want your friendship, don't make a nuisance of yourself. People don't really want to be friends'. This was mind-blowing for a young teenager. Many years later this particular person told me how devastated she was because she enjoyed our friendship, and wanted us to be together, sharing in mutual interests.

The example that I have just illustrated is when parental love goes too far, when they are making decisions for you such as what you will eat, what you will wear, who your friends will be, what time you will go to bed and what time you will get up in the morning. It should be that wherever possible, the person with a disability makes as many decisions for themselves as they can. A carer/parent should only be a facilitator to enable the disabled person to carry out their own wishes with the same level of confidentiality.

Now, all these years later, one of the most frequent remarks that I make to carers is; 'I make the decisions around here, even if they are the wrong ones'. I know that I am lucky because I am able to make rational decisions and I have to live, stand, or fall by the consequences of my actions. Everyone makes wrong decisions in their life from time to time, they may chose to buy an item of clothing, an expensive handbag, or equipment for a hobby and then decide they are not going to pursue it, but, that freedom of choice is the all-important issue. All too often, people who require care do not have freedom of choice, even when they are perfectly capable of doing so. Choices and the decision-making process are sometimes taken completely out of their hands.

Carers will say 'it's up to you' and then put up all the reasons why they can't or don't want to do something, so at the end of the day, there is no real choice or real freedom, because if the carer does not have a willing spontaneity to enable you to do something, then it won't happen. This is what happened to me so often in my teenage years and I always found myself backing down for a quiet life, rather than rocking the boat, because it was easier, but the frustration that I felt when I couldn't do the thing I wanted to do or I was told I couldn't spend a particular sum of money on something, was extremely galling even though I had the funds and the wherewithal. No-one has the right to control another human being in this way; the carers' role should be one of facilitation, they are my human facilitators, my enablers, who enable me to have a quality of life other than 'feeding and toileting'. It is difficult to put things in such stark terms, but this is the reality, this is what life and stultification is all about.

For someone who wants to be out there, experiencing what the world has to offer, it is hard when the people caring for you don't share the same interest and thereby the same enthusiasm to do something. In the end, the disabled person's life shuts down and they become depressed because they cannot pursue the things they want to, and they are not only trapped in a body, but trapped in the life they have to lead. Their home feels like a prison, maybe a luxurious one, but the need to break free becomes ever-more important. What one frequently hears is; 'You should be grateful for what you have, there are plenty of people far worse off than you'. I am fully aware that there are people far worse off, and I never stop 'being grateful' to others. However, an able-bodied person does not have to be grateful for going to the toilet or for being given a drink, they do these things spontaneously, yet I don't have a choice.

I can remember that one day I forgot to say thank you to my mother for tying my shoelaces. I then got lectured 'what do you think your last servant died of?' Her attitude has stayed with me all my life, this is why, now that I need care, I am meticulous about couching requests for help in an extremely polite way, trying to group things together that I need, or telling them in the order that I want particular tasks carried out, never forgetting to say 'would you be so kind as....', or thanking them, even when I am feeling particularly cross over something. The one problem that we have is that we cannot escape; other people can put their coat on, slam their front door and leave, if only for a short time, but we, as people with disability, are stuck with the awful frustration of wanting to escape, but not being able to; a recipe for a mind that feels explosive and creates nights of sleeplessness with the issues going round and round in one's head.

A Changing World

In 1965 I woke feeling that I had a migraine, the sky was bright yellow, and all the pavements were dark green. I was terrified.

I had time off school and after one week, returned, seemingly everything back to normal, then I found that I could see print, less and less. I was horrified, with a constant pain of anxiety in my stomach. What would this mean for me, and more importantly, what would it mean for my parents?

I did not want to put any extra pressure upon them. I kept what was going on with my eyes, to myself, for six months, but eventually I could no longer hide it. My mother was frantic with worry, and I was admitted to Moorfields eye hospital for examination under anaesthetic. My retina had detached in the one eye that I could see out of and I was told by a doctor sitting by my bedside, you will be blind within 3 months so you might as well get used to it. My mother couldn't take it in; it was terrible for me hearing her sobbing and screaming.

Detachments are very strange to live with. White objects presented a snow storm effect and the dark green and yellow colours were also still present. My mother said 'I'll be able to cope so long as you don't say "it isn't fair" and you want to be able to see'. Not being able to express your fears and feelings is an intolerable position to be in. I realise now she wasn't really thinking of me, but her own fears - she had to internalise everything that was happening. This is the one lesson that you quickly have to learn when dealing with a disabled person; one never knows how life can change from moment to moment. In the blinking of an eye your relatively stable world has been irrevocably turned upside down.

Carers must be ready to deal with those changes, but what I have found to my cost is that they do not like change; they want to hold on to what they know. I have frequently been criticised for changing the routine, it isn't that I am changing the routine for its own sake or to be bloody-minded, I am trying to keep up with changing events that may quite adversely alter my lifestyle. No-one wants to spend a long time in bed, being unable to move, but there are times when one does not have a choice. What I have learnt to my cost is that the only time we have, is now, because tomorrow could be very different. This would be a worthwhile lesson for all of us to learn, not just in terms of how we deal with disability and the ramifications of it, but for how we live our life in general.

Disability teaches you to live for the moment and value every single second. When further problems strike, some of which may be earth-shattering in proportion, one has to begin again; take stock of your life and keep going. There is no point in imagining what your life will be like in five-years' time.

My blindness meant that I had to go away to a boarding school for blind children, to be educated. Learning Braille was not easy; indeed it was one of the most challenging tasks I had to undertake. My local GP gave my mother good advice; 'whatever comes, meet it head on and get involved'. So she helped me when I was learning Braille and finding my way around the house. I knew the house like the back of my hand but I was terrified when it came to walking down stairs. It is very difficult for parents/carers to have a concept of 'blindness' and rarely put themselves in a position to think 'blind.' it is also absolutely essential that the carer, whoever they may be, just gets on and does things without a huge song and dance.

My mother had to do yet another double-take on the management of me, more and more time was taken up and she became ever more fearful and more possessive. She wanted to protect me from every little thing; it was suffocating. I know it sounds as though I am being terribly ungrateful; it isn't that, life is hard enough to keep hold of in this situation, for all parties, but mum had built her life around me and it was hard for me to be assertive, because to mum, assertiveness equalled ingratitude, but nothing could be further from the truth.

Every day of my life I have been conscious of how my situation affected the lives of others. My mum in particular, had had a really difficult life, losing her father and sister in the bombings of the East End in 1940. Doctors said that mum would never walk again, but they didn't reckon on her determination. She had both her legs in plaster for six months and a great deal of physiotherapy to follow. She, of all people, knew some of the struggle of my own life and she felt that she had been 'saved' to look after me. In her eyes, she had been chosen by God. Every time I went through agonising medical procedures, there was that identification and a growing bond between us, which meant that each of us knew something of the other's pain.

I was given a place at Dorton House School for the Blind, at Seal in Sevenoaks. Because the School authority was not prepared to do the physical caring, such as bathing and hair-washing, it necessitated my being a boarder from Sunday night until Friday, returning home at weekends; all the other students could care for themselves. Despite the pitfalls, I really grew and had breathing space for the first time in my life, and I truly blossomed. In two-and-a-half years, I found that my intellectual ability was recognised, perhaps for the first time in my life; passing flute examinations and O levels, none of which my family thought I was capable of achieving. For this two-and-a-half year period, my parents had time to be themselves, both sexually and emotionally, from Sunday to Friday, although, it did play on their minds how their child might be faring in a strange, unsighted environment. I have to say, I still did not see a lessening of the tension between them because of the fact that every weekend was still committed to driving me from London to Sevenoaks.

Dorton House no longer exists as a school, as there is no longer a need for specialist education; due to technology, most visually-impaired children can manage in mainstream education. What the school did for my parents was to show them that life still goes on, even when your child becomes blind, there is a case for living life to the full. I can remember one weekend when it was my birthday, having sixteen blind people home for the weekend. Sleeping so many was difficult, but we had great fun, with lots of music, guitar-playing and often very bawdy jokes which shocked the rest of our visitors. This was designed to make people aware of the normality of blindness. Certainly, it enabled my parents to feel much more relaxed about the whole situation; They knew I would make it somehow.

Mum came to love my friends from Dorton, and they in their turn liked her enormously, especially as she was such a good cook and homemaker. I was one of the privileged few who went home at weekends; some did not see their home from one term to the next, so to come home for two days to a family environment was great for them and made me more popular with the other kids at school.

I had the experience of my first boyfriend, shock - horror, how would mum cope with this? Answer: not very well. He could have been Prince Charles and it still would have been wrong; 'he's never going to care for you as I have done'. Again, the emotional blackmail rears its ugly head! Mum was never satisfied, being deeply critical of the man, speaking of his 'scruffy appearance' and 'shabby clothes and attitude.' She would never speak kindly and was always suspicious that I was being 'taken advantage of.' This was extremely hard to bear and lasted for five and a half years, with my boyfriend saying that he was breaking it off because he wanted to marry *me*, not my mother. This was a precursor for what was to happen to me in later life.

Any talk of freedom and independence, making one's own decision (even if wrong) was countered with 'after all I've done for you, and you treat me like this' – again, the level of emotional blackmail was intolerable. My mother could not see that she had made me the person I was. She had worked hard so that I could take my place in society and hold my head up high. I don't know why it is, but all too often I felt as though I had to apologise for being in this world, and for the inconvenience that I caused so many, because I wanted to strike out, breaking free of restrictions and live my life as normally as possible.

More than a Body

For most carers, helping the client to lead a 'normal life', is not part of their remit. It is about feeding, toileting, and keeping the person clean, and very little else. How sad it is, when your carer chooses not to share in any intellectual aspect of your life, such as books, music and theatre - all the things that make a person a whole, rounded individual. There is power within the caring relationship. As a counsellor of people with physical disabilities, I saw many examples where those caring for the disabled person, exerted control. If the carer does not want the client to do something, or go somewhere, all they have to do is to take longer over the usual routine, so that too much time has elapsed and it is now no longer possible to fulfil those wishes. All too often the carer will say 'it's a terrible day, raining heavily, cold and windy, I don't think you should go out, you might get a bad cold and then where will you be?' It didn't matter how often I pointed out that heavy head colds were not usually caused by cold weather, indeed I assumed that quite the opposite is true, a cold snap will often clear the head and make one feel a great deal better, away from the stuffiness of the house.

I had one incident of a young man in counselling, where he said he was never allowed to have his own pocket money. His parents did not want to be literally weighed down with carrying his money around and dealing with him. I'd never heard anything so ridiculous; this young man was perfectly capable. We talked around the issues of control for several sessions. Eventually he had the courage to confront his parents and they let him take control of his money, and decide what he wanted to do with his social services benefits and disability living allowance (now known as PIP, Personal Independence Payment). He opened a bank account for the first time and felt really 'grown up', deciding how much he should spend or save, and standing by those decisions. One week he came to see me in a really excited state, for he had saved his money over a period of months, then taken his family to the theatre and out to dinner. Both he and his family were very happy, and his mother and father in particular knew that their son was only too capable of making his own decisions. He needed to do this to prove a point; one small victory won, then he could move on and tackle the other questions to do with independent living, and to prepare himself should anything happen to his parents.

The fear of your carer or partner dying is ever present. When one tries to broach the subject, I am frequently told not to be morbid, 'they have years ahead of them'. Of course I pray that this is so, but the reality is that we simply don't know and the sense of bewilderment, confusion, and a feeling of total chaos is far harder to deal with than if the subject had never been raised.

I have been in a number of incidents where someone quite young and so-called able-bodied has died in front of me, absolutely shocking at the time and something you will never forget, but let's keep all these difficult questions under wraps and sweep them under the carpet in the hope that they will go away; sadly they will not.

When something happens, the disabled person has all the normal processes of grief to go through, as well as the terrible fear of what they will do now that they have lost a parent or partner. I can remember that I tried to talk to my parents along these lines, but was given very short shrift. I believe one of the hardest issues I have had to bear is the belief by my family and friends, that because I am in a wheelchair, my brains are quite definitely implanted into my backside. The assumption that, 'I do not know what I am talking about', is a very real one. People, sadly, do not take us seriously; so often, our views are regarded as nonsensical or inconsequential. Getting people to take you seriously is a very real problem, and I have realised, after having more than ten years of full time care, it is very difficult when a carer has to do very personal things for you, such as cleaning your backside, and then has to take you seriously as their boss.

The two issues do not go together. While they are doing highly personal things, they seem to find it impossible, especially when I have to come down hard on them over a particular issue. Often they pull faces (so people tell me), and just walk away. The transition from having help from parents, and latterly a husband, who gave their time and energy for free, to carers, who charge for almost everything, is extremely hard to bear. I see my life almost entirely within the context of being a feeding and toileting machine and a sort of 'automated cash machine.'

The real person has been submerged by all the care issues and the ramifications surrounding them. Those concepts of feeding and toileting and 'cash machines' do nothing for self esteem; one sees oneself as not much more than a commodity, a vehicle by which people can earn money. Often I have wondered whether I am really cared about by the people who look after me. In many instances, I am sure I am not; I want to be cared about, rather than cared for. There is a very definite distinction here, I want to feel that I matter to someone that they would care if I lived or died. There have been many times when I have felt that they did not, and this has left me with depression and a sense of great insecurity and loss. All my life I have been surrounded by people who I knew loved me (both my parents are now deceased), who would be there through thick and thin; now I am not so sure. Usually when life gets tough, the carers get going; when illness strikes, making the care role more difficult, one really finds out what the carers are made of.

Grasping what Life has to offer with both Hands

I ran a crisis counselling line for the leading disability newspaper 'Disability Now'. Many of the calls that I received were either from very worried parents, carers, or indeed from the people with disability themselves, regarding sexuality issues. Parents were worried about the development of their child and what this would mean for them, when seemingly there was little prospect of an outlet. The disabled people themselves find it incredibly hard to maintain any level of privacy. The able-bodied, on the other hand, have plenty of opportunity to titillate themselves in complete privacy with various items of literature and the internet. I have had many parents ring me to talk about their surprise and even sometimes disgust on finding that their disabled son has such explicit magazines. I have even had parents say that they would withhold the person's weekly pocket money if things such as this were going to be bought. I then focused on the normality of their child, saying that they should be grateful that the child has an outlet for such feelings.

This is all part of the independence process. The people with disabilities who are trying to feel their way in the world are often thwarted by the attitude of others. Any individual who is able-bodied does not have to 'air their dirty linen' in public but if the person has a disability, it is rare for their life not to have to be an 'open book' for very little is private or sacred. In the book, 'Entitled to Love' by Dr Wendy Greengross, she speaks about a mother who was deeply distressed when she realised that her son was masturbating, her answer to the mother about this was – 'make sure you leave a box of tissues close at hand, and a bag for the rubbish, and leave him to get on with it'.

I realise it is very hard for parents to tread this path, and learn to let go, but it is a natural part of living, helping their child to be a whole human being. The problem is, when to step back, and when to interfere, for interfering, it often is. Parents and carers often overstep the mark between what is solicitous and what is interference, particularly when they are governed by the rules of agency care.

Many, many times, a person with disability can be so frustrated because they have no means of self expression for fear that people will see the consequences of that expression and be angry, horrified, or upset, for example – masturbation or sexually-stained clothing.

I met the man who was to become my husband in 1985; we married in 1987 and had twenty-four-and-a-half years of a very happy marriage despite his subsequent illness, which greatly affected our lives together. Ralph was a father of two, and a grandfather of three. He lost his first wife to cancer. My mother was deeply watchful and disapproving of this relationship, and all through our marriage she gave her opinion whether it was sought, or not.

During courtship, I could never be free, wholly enjoying it for its own sake, because I needed help to go to bed. I was governed by a certain time. If we went out with friends to dinner, we would sometimes get a telephone call telling me to return home, because my parents wanted to go to bed. At the age of thirty-five, this was a bitter pill to swallow. I should have been allowed to make my own decisions, and behave like a responsible adult, and for people, whoever they were, to respect my position. After all, they never behaved like this with my able-bodied brothers!

I dreaded being put to bed by my mother because she would scrutinise my underclothing for any signs of sexual arousal. If she found any, then God help me, I was screamed and yelled at and had the underclothing jammed in my face. I hated this level of intrusion; this was taking the responsibility for a thirty-five-year-old far too far. It caused a great deal of tension between us. Why could she not be pleased that my body was functioning normally, and just discretely take the clothing away and put it in the washing machine, but sadly, this never happened.

It may be said that this was the irrationality of my mother, but I can tell you that she was not the only one who took the role of a carer beyond the confines of normal decency. It did nothing for our relationship; indeed, it made me very angry and resentful, no-one else in my family had this sort of treatment meted out to them. Fortunately I had a wonderfully understanding future husband who could not wait for our wedding day to arrive, to get me out of there.

This level of intrusion was a way of disempowering the disabled person beyond belief. I accept that parents have to be watchful and make sure that their child is not being taken advantage of but my advice would always be, sit back, watch, and make notes to discuss at a later stage if necessary, or just simply wait to see how the situation pans out, giving time for the couple to grow in love, or not as the case may be,together.

There is more than one way to disempower someone. It's quite simple really; just don't permit them to do any remotely dangerous task, such as using a sharp knife in the kitchen, never helping with daily tasks such as the washing and ironing. And as for being a home-maker, forget it. As my mother used to say 'Don't worry about how you look, because no-one is going to look at you!' - a total crushing of body image, and no opportunity to have confidence in one's appearance or one's ability to do certain tasks. In my case, I was kept wonderfully clean and tidy, but I was not dressed to kill, or stand out in a crowd. I had to put myself in the background. My mother was absolutely amazed when a very handsome able-bodied man took notice of me and loved me for my own self, warts and all. We had a wonderfully happy marriage for the first eight years until Parkinson's disease with Lewy Body Dementia struck him. Any striking out for independence, breaking the mould of domesticity was seen as ridiculous and stupid, because we should be saving for my future, when my husband was no longer around. Ralph was sixteen years older than me so the possibility that he may die before me was ever-present.

Because Ralph lost his first wife to cancer, his view was 'the only time we have is now', and we lived our life to the full and were ridiculously happy. We had a great sense of fun, people loved to be with us, and my social circle of friends was growing, it was fantastic. All those early years and the comments about not pushing myself forward, 'who do you think wants to be friends with you?' and any other negative thought you could think of, was suddenly stripped away, this life was for living, and I grasped it with both hands.

The phrase I loved most of all was whispered in my ear by my husband, gently mimicking my mother, when trying clothes on, 'And it's not practical', for this was a phrase that was uttered by my mother at every turn, killing thoughts that I might have had to strike out to be different. Ralph loved dressing me up for its own sake and for his sake. He wanted me to feel good as a woman, and look good just for me, and for him. It was truly fantastic; I had a real purpose for living for the first time in my thirty-seven years.

Up to now it had been hard work, pain, suffering, hospitalisation and invasive treatments. Ralph said, 'let's put some of that behind you, live for the moment and enjoy what comes'. We had many lovely weekends away in luxury hotels. This was one way he could be truly rested and looked after, being waited on hand and foot by someone else. We loved these three or four day trips to many different parts of England, wandering around like tourists, drinking in all that a particular area had to offer. One weekend in particular, going to Stratford upon Avon for a Shakespearean play, followed by a concert at Symphony Hall in Birmingham – what a feast of culture and a lovely time we had sharing together. One year, we had a musical Christmas with several concerts and a champagne reception each night thrown in for good measure, and of course we frequently returned to our favourite hotel in York, where we had our honeymoon. Ever the old romantics, we loved nothing more than to make each other happy.

The care role with all its needs and difficulties can be turned into something tender and loving. That concept is hard for people to take on board when one of the partners has a disability. Mostly they made comments such as 'does he know what he is taking on' and 'you are a nice person, but I could never take on board what Ralph has done'. Ralph's comment was, 'they don't know what they are missing'. I used to smile at him and say 'you are lovely', to which he would reply 'I mean it, and they really have no idea'. This was the kind of wonderful person he was, but sadly, people always assumed the worst, that he was out to take my money and property, then ditch me. Nothing could have been further from the truth and what we had, we built together.

Ralph was the physical powerhouse in the early part of our relationship, doing the driving, helping me set things up when I was preaching or lecturing and just being my eyes, arms and legs. I can remember one such lecture where, in the morning I was talking about loss and bereavement in terms of disability, and in the afternoon I was lecturing on the subject of sexuality and disability. I mused to the audience that it was the first time I was asked to speak on sex after death, which raised a laugh. Ralph thought it very important that I should have a complete change of outfit to also change the mood. This is how thoughtful he was, and it worked beautifully. Everything was fine for a number of years until Ralph's diagnosis of Parkinson's, subsequent knee replacements due to arthritis and then of course, the onset of advanced Parkinson's with Lewy body dementia. Then our lives changed dramatically.

First of all, Ralph deeply resented the fact that we had to have live-in carers whilst he was recovering from the knee surgery; a year in all. Then my problems started. I was no longer in control of my life; it was being controlled by others. One classic day when Ralph was beginning to walk with the aid of sticks, the carer came in one morning to wake me, and ask me what I wanted to wear that day. I decided that I would wear a cotton blouse with a pure wool suit. The carer's response was 'you can't do that, it's too hot and I will refuse to give it to you'. I was furious, but rather than create a scene, I just said 'well you pick something out of the wardrobe, and I'll wear it'. This she duly did. The next day, when I came out of the bathroom, Ralph was up on his sticks asking me what I wanted to wear. I laughed at him and said 'I'll wear the check cotton shirt with the navy blue wool suit'. He helped me to get dressed, then I called the carer. I'll never forget her response as long as I live; 'oh, you're wearing the clothes I told you that you couldn't wear'. I retorted that no one dictates to me what I will eat and what I will wear because I have so few choices in life. Later that day she apologised, telling me that I was absolutely right and that she was out of order. She certainly *was* out of order! The carer may think that they have complete control, but they definitely do not. I don't mind if the comments are negotiated but I hate it when I am told point blank what the carer is proposing 'to do' for me. Quite frankly, when someone has a good level of intelligence and the disabled person is able to fully articulate what they want or require, no one has the right to change it unless it is medically unsafe or dangerous. None of those issues apply in this case. My carer was a woman who had an over-inflated ego, believing that her voice should be heard at all costs and it was wrong.

This same carer had to attend a very important function in the presence of His Royal Highness The Prince of Wales. It seems that I would spend a great deal of time waiting for people to talk to me for one reason or another. There was a great deal of expectation buzzing around the room, wondering when HRH would arrive. Suddenly, my carer asks me very loudly and indiscreetly in front of some one hundred people, 'Do you want to go to the toilet, because I'd better take you now'. I was almost speechless which is quite rare for me and I made her remove me to the disability toilet area as quickly as possible. When I got in to the disability toilet, I said 'What the hell do you think you're doing out there?' She could not see the point I was making. So I spelt it out – extremely clearly. She still did not understand. So I had to say what you should have done was come to me and quietly ask whether I needed a comfort stop and we could have quietly left without anyone knowing the reason why I had temporarily withdrawn from the group. Later, I discovered that I had come second in the Health and Social Care Awards for that year with a £2,000 prize for my charity. There was naturally photographs taken of the happy occasion. My carer was absolutely determined that she would be in these photographs. She was a look-a-like of Camilla Parker-Bowles. Suddenly, she was standing behind me thrusting her face forward so that she would be fully in the picture. Again, I was not happy because, in a public situation such as I have just described, it is the duty of the carer to merge politely in the background until they are called for, or indeed, introduced to someone by myself. But the carer for that day did not understand social niceties and it is extremely difficult when people overstep the mark by placing themselves outside of their normal role, thereby inflating their ego. As a professional person, I have always found this very difficult because essentially, I am quite reserved when I have to be. I don't believe I ever go above my station – whatever that might be.

I can remember another incident with this same carer. We were involved with a charity street fair. There were all kinds of stall holders around and most importantly there was a very good Italian ice cream van, selling ice cream to the visitors. I asked her if she could get some for Ralph and I, and on her return I said 'and of course I meant you to have one too', 'that's all right, she said, 'I've taken the money out of your wallet'. There was no discussion, she had just taken charge. I hate it when people do things like that without my permission. I will very freely share. The sharing of what I have in my life is not a problem, and it only becomes one when people overstep the mark.

There was also the time when Ralph became tremendously frustrated because carers would just barge into our bedroom without knocking. This was difficult for us as a couple because Ralph and I found it better to be close in the morning when Ralph was not suffering from fatigue. All of a sudden the door would be flung open without warning, so one day he said to the carer, 'I want you to go to Waitrose and then I want you to go to Tesco'. She retorted, 'but I can get all these things in the one supermarket, why do you want me to go to two?', He said, 'because I want to give my wife a cuddle without interruption, now please leave us alone'. She laughed, and I think, got the message, namely, that privacy must be respected.

It is very difficult for carers when there are two people in the house. Mostly they don't like being part of a family unit, their response is often, 'I am only paid to help one person, not two'. Carer's attitudes often created more domestic tension, which wasn't good. Every couple has times when they want to express their feelings to one another over something that irritates them, but when your home is invaded by carers, this is very hard to keep control of, and of course, there are times when it overspills, and the carers are party to the tensions between you. Not good but almost inevitable unless you are a superhuman couple!

I had one very good carer from an agency; she was my carer, in fact, for six-and-a-half years. She was one of the few people that went the extra mile. We both loved music and she would frequently take me to concerts and we were quite close. I know that she used to worry about us when she had to leave, life was always a struggle and as Ralph's Parkinson's advanced, it became a nightmare. I never knew what scrapes we would get into and the tension was almost unbearable.

The worst day's work I ever did was to give my care over to an agency. The only good thing about it was that you were guaranteed not to be left stranded. However, so often, it wasn't a case of matching a person to a carer, which of course should be the ultimate goal, it was merely a case of putting a body to a body and not much else. Very few had a good command of the English language, so there was always a cultural barrier, and very often, a language barrier that was all the more intimidating because of my blindness. If I had been sighted, I would have understood what they were asking by getting them to point or show me the object that they were trying to pronounce. I have had many bad experiences where my attitude of concern towards a carer was misconstrued. I was asked, 'what was my hidden agenda?' and told 'no-one is as kind as you; you must have an ulterior motive'. The only ulterior motive I ever had was to try and make a person feel welcome, at home, and wanted. Sadly, I was taken advantage of many times, and I had items stolen from my home, from right under my very nose. They would put things in their cases and just nonchalantly say goodbye as they left, knowing that they would probably never be returning, and that they were safe because the missing items would only be discovered when another carer came on duty. One such incident was with a brand new duvet, which came in two parts that you clip together to give you a thicker tog-rating for the winter. As many of my carers came from hot countries, they always seemed to feel the cold. One part of this duvet was still in its wrapping, waiting for the very cold weather, when the carer who always felt the cold, came on duty. She went to the wardrobe to get this duvet and found it was missing.

I feel what bothers me about all of this is not so much the cost of the item, although combination duvets are not cheap, but the mere fact that they can take it from my home, with such impunity that due to my blindness, their crime would go undetected for quite some time. I feel betrayed by them because they have taken full advantage of my blindness, and laughed behind my back. I have lost beautiful pieces of cut glass and other items from a display cabinet. This makes me particularly sad as they were specialist pieces purchased by my husband and I, and therefore felt irreplaceable.

I had another incident where one particular carer used to make telephone calls on my landline to Africa whilst I was in the bath. She counted on my never checking of the bill, but she forgot that I was a fairly astute person and had some idea of what the size of my telephone bill should be every quarter. When I saw the dramatic increase, I looked further into the matter with my secretary; we found that there had been many calls made to Africa - £130 worth in fact. I immediately telephoned the care agency, who questioned me on who I thought had done this. I stated that the calls corresponded to the weeks that this particular carer was on duty. I was asked by the care agency to send a copy of the bills; they too did a similar check and immediately dismissed the person, and took the value of the telephone calls from her salary.

I can remember one particular day because it was Friday the 13th; I asked the carer on duty if she was suspicious about such a day. She replied 'Friday the 13th doesn't' make any difference to me'. She was to learn to her cost that it did. I had spoken to my bank manager about the difficulties I had with carers drawing cash from my account, and dealing with any other transactions, because at this point in my life I did not always have carers who could drive, and therefore I could not get to the bank. Certain safeguards were put in place due to my blindness, and my bank and credit cards were under special scrutiny. On this particular day, a carer came back from shopping saying that she would never go into the bank for me ever again, ' They weren't very nice, and they were racist,' she said. She started to cook herself some concoction for lunch, when suddenly there was a knock at the door and a neighbour came in and told me that there were two policemen with panda cars, wanting to talk to me. They had been contacted by the bank regarding irregularities with my account. The carer in question was questioned by the two policemen. They told me that they would be doing some checks and be contacting me later. In the meantime I could hear frantic conversation on the telephone with very raised, excited voices, though naturally, due to the carer speaking in her native tongue, I could not understand what was being said. Sometime later the policeman returned telling me that they were going to arrest my carer. My response was,

'You can't do that.'

'Why not?' the policeman said.

'Because I haven't been to the toilet,' I replied. The policeman said, 'We will allow her to take you to the toilet but you must leave the door fully open and there will be three policemen standing in your hallway.'

I was absolutely horrified; she attempted to close the toilet door but it was kicked open by the policeman in the hallway. When she was charged and taken away by the police, I rang the care agency and said 'I'm going to make your day!' When I told them what had happened they were absolutely incredulous. The police did not care whether I had a meal or could manage.

Their main consideration was to get this woman out of my way. I called a neighbour who helped me to prepare a meal and I got a friend to come and be with me overnight. I was becoming increasingly disillusioned by agency care. I suppose the answer was to look for another agency, but they were one of the least expensive around, and known to social services. When the case came up at the local court, I was not required to attend; she pleaded guilty and was given a small fine. I don't know whether she lost her job as well.

One always has to be careful of giving your carers the whereabouts of what you are doing with your life, and at what time. The person who got arrested for dubious dealings at my bank, naturally went off duty and did not return. One week later when my usual carer was on duty, I heard the front door open, but she didn't come into the room. I rang her number to see where she was, she was in fact in a taxi, on her way back to the house with my shopping. I had the distinct feeling that someone was sitting on the chair behind me, I swung my chair round, and asked who was there and got no response, and this feeling of human presence did not go away. Then I heard footsteps across my office and the toilet being used adjacent to the office. I then heard them run out of the room quickly, and the front door close. I rang the local police station, expressing my concern, and an officer came round to see me. They had on record the incident from the previous week. On speaking to the care agency, their response was, 'You're obviously feeling anxious, perhaps it was Harvey (my spaniel) walking across the floor.' My response was, 'Yes, but he can't flush the toilet, can he?' That night the young lady in question telephoned asking me how I was and, whether I had been out to lunch with my friend today. That made me all the more suspicious because she had no reason to call. I suspect she had given somebody a key, and they thought it was safe because I wasn't meant to be there.

Naturally, after this incident, all the locks on my house were changed, which was quite a costly affair.
There were many incidents like this, and I have to say, it does little for your faith in human nature. I was battling with my own disability, pain and loss of my husband, for indeed it was a form of loss once he went into a care home, yet I suffered still further with a sense of disbelief and incredulity that people, who are supposed to be carers, could treat another human being in this way.

I have often felt that there is an underlying issue of racism; so many carers level the fact that they think you are racist towards them, when in fact, nothing could be further from the truth. What I level at them, is their appalling behaviour towards another human being, who is already disadvantaged. They do not need further marginalisation meted out to them by care workers. Sometimes I wonder where some of the people come from and how they are given the appointments. There is an attitude by certain members of society who say, 'if you can't get a job, be a carer.' What people don't realise is, that to be a carer demands patience, understanding, kindness, thoughtfulness, and of gritting the teeth when the client is particularly difficult.

When the only person with me is a carer, I have to put in place certain safeguards, namely, that cheques are not written for me to sign without another person overseeing the amount, and that money in my wallet is regularly checked against expenditure. This is quite a difficult area, because one does not want a person to be party to everything you spend or do. There is of course a rule of confidentiality that I try to enforce within my own home, but sadly carers have been known to overstep the mark, telling my family members what I have spent on a piece of jewellery for example, which has nothing to do with them, or anyone else. This was my own personal choice, and I was totally capable of making it. This certain family member quoted the exact price of this piece of jewellery down to the last penny, so I knew that the information had been passed on. I made it abundantly clear to the carer, that what goes on in my home, stays in my home, and does not go outside. Of course there would always be an exception, namely if there was any abuse or improper behaviour meted out to the client by another carer, or indeed, if I myself, being the client, was abusive or violent towards the carer. Improper behaviour is not just about physical or sexual abuse, it is about somebody taking full advantage of my blindness and/or lack of physical movement. For example, one such carer would do the shopping and when I queried the amount that she had spent, her answer was, 'things are so expensive these days.' One day my brother came to visit, he said 'What are all these sweet things such as cake, doing in the fridge, when you are supposed to be dieting?' I told him that I had not bought these things, but he would not hear of my explanation, not that it had anything to do with him anyway. Life should be about making one's own choices, whether they are right or wrong. He told me the number of cakes that were in my fridge. I was incredulous, they were nothing to do with me, and however, if a person is going to be devious, and downright untruthful, they have to have a good memory; the carer in question did not. I got someone to read me the last grocery bill. Sure enough all the cakes that were in my fridge, were also on the bill, together with dog food and chicken breast that I hadn't ordered. I approached the carer regarding these items; her response was that she had given me the wrong bill. I said, 'do you think I could have the right one?', but it was not forthcoming. I wondered how many food bills I had paid for in this way, and from then on, I always had someone check the bills. She was being paid privately by me, and not through an agency. I found it incredibly hard to get carers on a regular basis, and usually got them through recommendation from other carers, which I know can be fatal, but this was all done at a time when I was very new to all the care issues, and exceedingly fearful for my future.

I had a Suffolk care agency for something in the region of eight to nine years. There were three girls, Pumi, Pat, and Mercy who were the best of a very poor bunch, so much so, that the owner of the agency allowed me to take all three girls as my private carers. This worked well for some six-and-a-half years when circumstances changed. I'd had a really rough ride at the hands of people who should never be doing care and I vowed that things would have to change so I engaged people on a private basis with social services meeting some of the costs and my funding of the rest. All worked ok until my money ran out – or at least, was running out. There was one such privately engaged carer who thought that I was a soft touch. It was Christmas time and she was engaged over the Christmas period until something like the 12th of January. I had some friends staying in a nearby hotel and we had decided to go to a restaurant for good quality fish and chips. On arrival, the carer tipped my chair up a kerb and hurt her hand doing so. She had advised me previously that the handle bar grip on my chair was faulty – I told her how to deal with it, namely, to spray the handle with hair lacquer and then, pushing the grip onto the chair handle so that it would stick. However, she decided that she would not bother with this – it was perfectly manageable if the carer put their hand at the top of the grip so that it could not move but she unfortunately, held the grip at the bottom so that it fell off and jarred her hand as she went up the kerb. All that evening she bitterly complained and then did not allow me to go to church so my friend, who was a driver, drove all the remaining people to church but not my carer. After three days of moping around she said that she would have to go home. Currently, I have now found out that I am being personally sued for something that she neglected to do. The figure as I write is up to £27,000 – a rather expensive handle bar grip! During that period when she was helping me to prepare for guests who were coming to stay she was doing rather a lot of shopping/Christmas shopping. When I asked her what the bill was she would not tell me, saying, you don't really want to know do you? Of course I wanted to know and I got more and more concerned as the time went on. Eventually, I managed to get someone to take me to Waitrose and log into my Waitrose account. I asked someone at the desk to give me a copy of my bill then I went to Tesco's and did the same. Eventually those bills were faxed to me. I found to my absolute horror on investigating that she had spent over £500 on shopping and that didn't include meat that I would use. I had a turkey and all the trimmings arriving on Christmas Eve. There were many items on this bill that I did not purchase such as cat food, chicken breasts, dog biscuits, and five one-pound bars of Cadbury's fruit and nut chocolate. I thought it was a cast iron case for nailing this person with her dishonesty but sadly I was wrong. I called my local police and explained. He looked at the items one by one and there were many that I had no knowledge of. His response was sadly "I believe you Lin, but I am afraid it is your word against hers."

A policemen was then assigned to visit her in Yorkshire where she lived. All these different items especially cat food (I don't even own a cat), large bars of chocolate and other goodies were not part of my equation. The issue was taken to the police superintendent for his take on the matter and his response was again, that it was only my word against hers. If people are allowed to be deceitful then where is the hope for all of us? Although I feel very hurt and angry, it was not really worth pursuing.

A Role Reversal

My husband's care needs were becoming more and more advanced to the extent that I had to place him in a residential care home. I had weeks of negotiation with the local authority as to a suitable care home, not just for Ralph's needs, but for mine too from the visiting point of view. Weeks of pressure and tension, probably, if I'm honest, was too much for one person to have to cope with. The day dawned for Ralph to be transferred from hospital into the care home. There was much preparation, and he was due to arrive around lunch time. I was incredibly weepy that day, feeling so guilty about having to place him into a care home, but his requirements were becoming impossible for me to manage at home. All that day I tried to get over to the care home. The carer on duty was refusing to take me, and then, when Ralph's daughter visited and was sewing name tags onto his clothing, I asked if she would come with me and assist me into the home, if I ordered a taxi. She didn't think it would be a good idea because it would be too emotional – if I'm honest, I'm not really sure which of us that applied to! I had worked relentlessly over the last few weeks to get Ralph established in a home that should meet his needs. At first, the room he was put into was very small, indeed you could barely swing a cat in there, if you pardon my expression. This was changed some six months later when Ralph was given a ground floor room with a patio garden overlooking the lawns and trees. This was a much better outlook for him as he greatly enjoyed watching the antics of the squirrels as they swung from one branch to another to enable them to get down and take the nuts out of the nut-holder. But the squirrels were more ingenious, they not only shook the holder but they also pulled on the bottom of the container so that all the nuts fell onto the ground then the squirrels literally 'squirreled' them away, burying them for future use. But for now, Ralph and I had to deal with our individually hurt feelings – he feeling rejected, me feeling guilty and as though I had been battered with a battering ram, not knowing which way to turn.

Apart from feeling absolutely dreadful, I also had the frustration of people dictating to me and controlling my life to the extent that I could not do what I wanted to do. This was grossly unfair and a step too far. All I could do was send Ralph a dozen red roses with a message of love on them, telling him that I would be there soon. I rang and spoke to him and he was very angry that I was not at the home to help him settle in. I assured him that this was beyond my control and that had I had a choice in the matter, I would have been there. Ralph could not see my dilemma, 'you are my wife, and I expect you to be here. In fact you are the only person I want here'. That comment made me feel even worse. All of us have an experience of grief at some point in our life, be it a partnership or the loss of a husband or wife. I think those people who are partners of someone with dementia that is in its latter stages probably suffer more hardship than most. It is so hard when there is no recognition coming back as to who you are. Fortunately, Ralph knew who I was right to the end although he did have these periods where he was totally confused, very irrational, and unresponsive. It is so difficult to have to steel yourself to go into the home being as bright and cheerful as you possibly can when there is virtually nothing coming back. You long for a good day where you can have a conversation that is meaningful. Knowing what it's like for dementia patients, I would try and focus on the good things within our relationship. It was utterly devastating when Ralph said how much he wanted me there yet due to carers taking control because they thought it would be better for me not to see him in a distressed state I felt devastated and I also believe that they had no right to make that decision. The care home, however, has a policy which is that the loved ones do not visit for the first forty-eight hours to allow the new patient to settle. Ralph was never going to cooperate with that, indeed it made him all the more angry and determined to protest and make life more difficult for me.

I had one carer from Eastern Europe. She was a lovely person, and over the weeks and months I had really come to love her. She was tremendously excited because her daughter was expecting her first child. Chatting one day, she said how difficult it was to get good quality toys in her country of origin. I went to one of our local villages and purchased two lovely teddy bears, one in pure white, the other in traditional brown colours. I also had a friend make a baby shawl, and sent them abroad. I later heard that this carer said that I tried to bribe carers to stay; nothing could be further from the truth and I felt deeply hurt and insulted by the comment.

My husband had been in the care home for some four-and-a-half years when sadly, he passed away. I was totally devastated; I coped with my grief and all the arrangements for his funeral with the help of my secretary and no support from my family. It was perhaps the most trying time of my life, not helped by a change of carer, from a care agency almost every week; it was a totally shattering experience, having to train someone week after week is truly exhausting. I desperately needed some mental peace, but sadly I did not get any. I felt that if I was continually put under this kind of pressure, I would have a breakdown. The more pressure I was under, the more certain carers put the screws on, making my life even harder to bear. I tried desperately to make things as nice as I could; I had told the care agency that I would not be sticking to the five pound rule for a Christmas present, as I was in a position to give the carers something decent. I arranged for the girls to have gold earrings that I had chosen and got the jeweller to box and wrap them individually with very pretty ribbon. One girl's response was, 'What makes you think I want to receive a gift from you?' I was devastated, but took the rejection on the chin and still managed to keep my manners even though it was pretty near impossible. Indeed, as my husband was dying, he asked me to provide thirty-seven presents for the carers who had looked after him. I am sure that not many people have had that responsibility at such a difficult time.

Carers so often know no boundaries. I had a nineteen-year-old carer who suddenly said, 'What I want to know is, how did you and your husband manage to 'do' it?' I was incredulous, and responded, 'What arrangements my husband and I came to was our own private affair, and you have no right to ask such questions, that is pushing your "need to know" too far.' The following day she took a pound of sausages out of my refrigerator, put them in my hand as she walked past, and said, 'What does this remind you of?' I rang the agency and they were absolutely gobsmacked. They said she would finish the week up and not be coming back. I said that I felt that this young lady was in need of social grooming.

The consequences of the lack of success with carers, was that I became totally lacking in self-confidence, doubting my own ability, and feeling that I did not want to wake up in the morning. Indeed, I did not care whether I lived or died. I was just so exhausted from all the burdens placed upon me. People know about the rudiments of care, but sadly, they have no understanding of Cerebral Palsy Quadriplegia and the pain therein. I was frequently told that I did nothing but complain, 'You, you're always in pain.' The fact of the matter is, I am in pain all the time, to a lesser or greater extent. When my pain was particularly excruciating, I didn't know that I was suffering from a vitamin D deficiency, the consequence of which is to give one acute pain that strikes without warning on any part of the body along with extreme fatigue, and general exhaustion. One should have a level of 75 in the body for vitamin D, mine was just 15. I discovered this through listening to Dr Mark Porter on a Radio 4's casebook programme about vitamin D. On that programme was a lady who thought she was suffering from acute arthritis. She was in so much pain that she had to give up her job as a secretary, due to pains in her arms, hands and knees. The only way doctors realised she had vitamin D deficiency, was because pain-killing medication did not ease the problem. At that time I was in exactly the same position. I was taking up to eight tablets a day with hardly any respite; I even attended a pain clinic. However, the carers had no understanding and just saw the way that I yelped or cried with pain, as just being difficult. 'We cannot do anything right', they said. I realise how it must have seemed, but I was powerless to do anything about it because I was so ill. It was only when I collapsed on the floor after a bout of flu, and had no strength to help myself, that they realised something was wrong. If I had been the type to complain all the time, they would have got the message, but because I kept so much of my pain to myself, they had no idea how seriously ill I was.

I think that one of the things I find most difficult, is that carers rarely use their initiative, and by and large don't care how they treat your home; things always have to be repaired or replaced because of heavy-handedness. Simple things such as placing cutlery in a drawer becomes an incredibly noisy operation, chucking knives, forks, and spoons in with a heavy hand, one by one. The concept of drying all the forks, putting them in one pile and then placing them in the drawer together gently, is beyond them.

I am meticulous in everything that I try to do. Carers watch me preparing vegetables and peeling satsumas, taking off every tiny bit of pith and they are amazed at my patience. I suppose it has much to do with the way blindness teaches you patience. For example, when carers wash my hair, I am usually soaking wet, but when I do it myself, I use the two-flannel method, just putting the cloth in the water, squeezing it to get rid of excess water then running it through my hair until it is free of soap. I do this so carefully, that I can remain fully dressed, without spilling anything. Carers can't believe that it is possible to do this, but I point out that it's all about being careful. I always wash the bottle of shampoo and rinse the bathroom sink and

I am also very careful with the use of the hairdryer. It isn't necessary to blow the wet hair all over your face, if you keep the hairdryer close to the head and brush it into shape as you go.

If I were physically capable, my home would be as bright as a new pin, and always spotlessly clean. I am meticulous about personal hygiene and making sure that my clothing is spotlessly clean. I never want concessions because of disability. I have to work all the harder to make things come right, this is why my personal care regime takes so long. Many carers feel that I am unnecessarily fussy, but as someone who is frequently in the public eye in a lecturing capacity, I must know that I am properly presented; also my mother would never forgive me if I did not try to maintain standards! Quite naturally there are times when it all goes horribly wrong, and you need help to clean up and change clothing if necessary. Fortunately, these incidents are not too common.

Most of us do not think about the consequence for someone who needs hoisting (as I do now), yet they wish to lead a normal life (whatever that might mean). If one can't use a toilet, one is then forced to only go out for a maximum of four hours so that one can get to the toilet. That means that work activity and socialisation such as going for a meal and a concert is completely out of the question. I live some seventy-five miles from the City of London, which means I leave my home at around three and get to London before the rush hour. In reality this means ten hours without going to the toilet; it really is a case of London is happy to welcome you, but you must take your urine home with you. Thankfully, the position is beginning to change. More and more there is a new form of public disability toilet called 'Changing Places.' These are specially designed for people who need to be hoisted and they also have a 'Closomat' toilet which is a toilet that washes and dries. This innovation has now meant that I can go to London and enjoy wonderful classical music concerts again. I have only been hoisted for some three years, which

I thought was the end of my life, and I was deeply distressed by it. The worst side of it is that one has to remove one's underclothing before being hoisted onto the toilet; it cannot be pulled down in the conventional way because the sling goes round your whole body. It takes as many as six lifts of the hoist to take you from bed to chair, to toilet, back onto the chair, back onto the bed to replace clothing then finally off the bed into the wheelchair. At the end of all this I am exhausted.

People who do not understand disability have no concept about working to routine; mostly I am not ready to receive visitors until 11am unless pre-arranged. The Methodist Church that I attend is some fifteen-miles from my home. Of course, there are others, but this is the church I choose to worship in. This means starting my day at 6.15 on a Sunday morning, having only a hydration drink and arriving at church for 9.30, and leaving just after 11. For the rest of the congregation, this is a simple task; they do not have to cope with problems such as graciously refusing several cups of tea, and not being able to stay longer at the end for social events. There is not the luxury of a Changing Places toilet, so therefore my socialisation is dramatically curtailed.

No-one chooses to have to live like this, it is incredibly frustrating, and realistically no-one would choose to have carers living in their home twenty-four-seven. This is not being disrespectful to the carers in any way, but all of us choose who we wish to live with, and although there will be times when one wishes one's family to be as far away as possible, the fact of the matter is that the able-bodied members of the family have a choice. If your family or friends don't help you, the only choice you have left is to be covered in urine or excrement very quickly, so even if there is a clash of personality or misunderstanding, it's often the case of 'the better the devil you know, than the one you don't.' Having no choice is what creates the frustration, and bad quality carers makes me feel that I am bad also, which is not right. The carer's role should be to enhance the life of the individual that they care for, making them feel that they are cared about, and valued by those who care for them. After all, they are the ones who are being paid, we are not holding a gun to their head saying that they must be a carer; that is a choice that they have freely made without any duress on our part.

I always say to carers that I am deeply grateful to them for some of the things that they have to do, and in all honesty, I don't know if I could do them myself. However, it is very difficult when one is thrown together with a person you would not choose to live with under normal circumstances, and the situation is, that you have no choice. Even going into a care home would not necessarily solve the problem. I feel sure that the only difference is that there would be more people to relate to if there were a clash of personalities, and of course that would be extremely useful.

My philosophy on life is that I try to make the most of every God-given moment; I love nothing more than to be able to go to London concert venues and listen to many international artists of world - renown. I wrongly assumed that the majority of my carers would like the opportunity to do the same; I find that it is incredibly difficult to get them to come out of their comfort zone and have a new experience. I have one carer who really enjoys listening to classical music. Her family think it rather strange, but what I am pleased about is that she goes on regardless. She loves the Beethoven piano concertos and the nine symphonies, the Pastoral being her favourite. Now she has familiarised herself with these and they have become second nature, she wants to learn more. I am absolutely thrilled by this; it is my belief that one has to be shown the right music at the right time. What a privilege to share in such moments of giving people a wonderful treat. This is a rare occurrence, but when it happens, it's fantastic. Music is my life; it is my paintbrush on the world. Just lately I have a new carer who is wildly enthusiastic about music, and we share it in equal passion. This carer has opened up my life in a way that I would not have dreamed possible; how one person can make a difference. It is not just about 'feeding and toileting'.

As I have said, one person can make a dramatic change for the better; equally one person can also change things for the worse. One would not believe it possible that in the space of three days, one could feel that your life was totally worthless due to the attitude of a carer. By the end of this particular three days I was at the point of collapse, phoning the emergency number of the care agency at 6am. I had battled, and I use that word in its correct context, with this particular carer since Tuesday, and by the Friday I was on my knees, simply unable to cope, quite frankly feeling totally terrified at what this person might mete out to me. I am not sure whether she could not understand English or just had no desire to help. Either way, I was tearing my hair out.

If the carer's comprehension of the English language is so poor that either you cannot understand them, or they cannot understand you, then the care agency has a very real problem that they are not addressing, namely, their duty towards the client. I speak very clear English and give my instructions very concisely, but in this particular case, I too could have been speaking a foreign language. None of what I requested was going in, and we were both getting extremely exasperated and frustrated with one another. It transpired that this person seemingly did not know how to cook; she wanted me to provide take-away food or have sandwiches for my main meal. When one day I asked her to roast a chicken, several hours went by and I did not hear any activity in the kitchen, she kept telling me that she had put the chicken in the oven, but I could not smell it cooking and I stated to her that she had not done it. She took a pan out of my oven drawer, slammed the chicken onto it, and put it in the oven. Still I could not smell it cooking. That night I went to bed hungry because no food had been provided, even though I had prepared all the vegetables for her. I went to bed feeling very frustrated because I was angry that the care agency had provided me with someone so incapable. It is tremendously important when the client is visually impaired, that the carer is fully aware of the client's needs, and capable of executing them. This carer was obviously not!! I got her to help me into bed, and I asked her to raise the nightdress so that it would not impede me when I was rolling over. She did not know the difference between 'raising' the nightdress and 'lowering' the nightdress, and in the end, feeling totally frustrated, I took hold of my nightie and said 'This is up,' raising it above my knees, 'And this is down,' lowering the nightdress. I was definitely speaking in an unintelligible language as far as she was concerned.

I lay there all night thinking of what was to come the following day. I was shaking with fear. In the end I was so exhausted, I could barely move. At five in the morning, I rang my cleaner who knew my needs exceedingly well, and asked her to come and rescue me, which she duly did. She arrived at 6am, getting me out of bed, putting me in and out of the bath and helping me to get dressed. Eventually somewhere near 9 o'clock, the carer arrived in the bathroom saying, 'Oh, you're up, I thought I heard a noise.' Sadly she had not come to investigate. I asked for a meeting that afternoon with care-agency staff. They asked my previous carer to return early, to look after me. When she arrived, later that day, her reaction was 'You poor darling, what have they done to you? When I left you on Tuesday, you were bright and happy? Now you look totally grey and on the point of collapse.' She was absolutely right about that, I had struggled so much during those three days, feeling completely exhausted, that I had no energy left to go over the same things again and again.

Everyone thinks that having a twenty-four-seven carer is wonderful. For the most part, nothing could be further from the truth. For me, it is totally shattering when one is repeating the same scenarios over and over again. It's even harder when one feels that one is not listened to by your carer because they have a set view on how they wish to do things and what they expect. Anything that takes them out of their comfort zone, which is not in the normal way of doing things, or beyond the usual expectations, is at best, frowned upon, and at worst, meets with a total refusal to comply with my wishes. Caring is much more than feeding and toileting. I cannot emphasise this nearly enough. Like the situation with the carer who did not cook the chicken, and indeed many other aspects of that three days, I was left being reported on and had criticisms of me that were completely unfounded. So often I am left wondering what I should do – perhaps I try to make people too happy and am too welcoming. There is not enough demarcation between my being their boss because they want everything to be a doddle so that they can just sail through life from morning to night.

The Emotional Side of Caring

Coping with new carers, for what is known as shadowing, is an exhausting experience for the client, particularly when the carer has no idea how to care. So often we are let out to another human being and we are on a wing and a prayer as to whether it is going to be successful. I have to say that usually one can tell within the space of a couple of hours as to whether it is going to work or not. Some carers just think that I am being difficult, when in fact all I am trying to do is live my life as closely as possible to that of an able-bodied person. The only problem is that I need help to achieve it.

I have had so many things happen to me, hence the reason for writing this book. One such privately engaged carer, to my horror, had a bad case of head-lice. The first I knew of it was when my hairdresser asked me if I had been near any children lately. My response was 'No, but I know who I have been near.' My hairdresser went and spoke to her. Her response was, 'I don't know what all the fuss is about, they are quite friendly little creatures.' I was absolutely frantic, all she was using to get rid of them was hair conditioner, which of course did not solve the problem. This was the one time when I really lost it. Her response was to approach me from behind and hit me with a rolled-up tea towel as hard as she could across the eyes. I was incredibly worried about this, and vowed that if ever my eye surgery site broke down, I would take this as far as I could. I rang my friend who said that she would come and help, but I must now involve an agency. I was so distressed, that I started to have boils appear on my body. One on the back of my leg was as large as a fifty-pence piece, and it was in line with the edge of the wheelchair seat. I arranged a visit from a local agency who gave me a detailed assessment regarding movement and needs. This whole process was extremely distressing, partly because it makes one realise how difficult the various procedures are. Not least of all because one quickly realises how restricted you are, and at the mercy of carers.

My first carer from the agency stayed in her room for much of the time. I sat in my kitchen, listening to the radio but not knowing what I should do about the pain of the boil on the back of my leg. It was like a raging tooth ache. I asked the carer if she would mind staying with me for a while, because I did not feel very well. She declined my invitation. Later that evening, when the throbbing sensation was at its height, I suddenly felt a popping sensation, and suggested to the carer that she better come and check me out. She said I would be fine and not to make a fuss, but on entering the bathroom, she realised that I had been telling the truth, because as I stood, the blood started to ooze out from my leg and everything was in an awful mess.

As this was my first introduction to agency care, I was not impressed. A temporary plaster was applied overnight, and the doctor was called in the morning. This boil had left such a hole, that I needed to have the district nurses come every day to pack the wound; this was not a nice experience. It was only a matter of weeks before this carer left.

Up to now, I have given examples of care that has not been fit for purpose so to speak, therefore, I would like to balance up this book by writing about those who've provided a good level of care and one who has been absolutely superb and the epitome of how care should be done in a professional and exemplary way. I have had four African carers who supported me through a very difficult period in my life – firstly, when my husband died and latterly when I had a malignant carcinoma of my womb. These four people were there when medical examinations were difficult and we had a life-threatening situation where I subsequently had my womb and both ovaries removed. Before my surgery I had drugs to control the bleeding but on speaking to my surgeon he told me that the tumour was enlarging, heading towards the outer lining of my womb. When I asked what would happen when it reached that point he said 'Well, it's anyone's guess and it depends on what will be the limiting factor of your life.' I had an extremely good rapport with my surgeon and told him that he'd better get on with the job of removing the tumour. He was reluctant to do this because I had other complications of a massive hiatus hernia which could have caused me great problems with the anaesthetic. He told me that I had a one in four chance of dying on the operating table as opposed the normal response of one in a thousand. I retorted 'Well if I have a one in four chance of dying, that means, I have a 75% chance of living.' Whilst I was in his consulting room, a nurse suddenly put a chair next to me and linked her arm in mine. The surgeon wanted me to go away and think about the issues over the weekend. I refused and asked for him to just give me the papers and let me sign them and arrange for me to be admitted for the procedure. I turned to the oncology nurse sitting next to me and patted her hand saying 'It's alright – you can let go now and I won't fall on the floor.'

Both she and the surgeon said that they thought that I was remarkable. Whether I was remarkable or not, did not come into it – I just wanted the issue dealt with so that I could move on. On leaving the consulting room I was faced with my carers waiting outside 'Why do you look so serious,' they said. I explained what happened. I expected a comforting hand on the shoulder or a hug but it did not happen – probably because they were feeling quite shocked and we went a couple of weeks before admission. On entering the hospital I had been placed in a side ward so that my carers could assist me – the surgeon believing that it would be better for me to have people close by that I knew. I had quite a difficult time and had to spend eight days on oxygen which wasn't easy. My carer called 'Mercy' would take me to the chapel so that I could pray and take part in the church services. At one time, I fell asleep and she woke me very gently to say that we should leave. Those four African carers worked on a two-day on, two-day off basis, giving me round the clock assistance when it was necessary. Thankfully, all has been well up until now although I realised only too well how my life can change when cancer is in the equation. I have had many incidents in my life when one would have been knocked out by the blows that I have encountered but I have been blessed with great determination and a spirit that doesn't often get too downcast. So one keeps going and hoping that life will be different.

For almost two years I had a group of three carers who supported me through difficult times. There was an incident when I had an infection which necessitated hospital treatment. This took the form of a plug in both ears with antibiotics and antifungal treatment. This rendered me almost totally deaf for eleven weeks whilst the treatment was taking effect. As I mentioned earlier, I am totally blind and partially deaf, normally using two hearing aids but during this period hearing aids could not be worn. I have never felt so cut off in all of my life and I was terrified for the whole of that time. My carer, Melody, was truly marvellous in helping. It necessitated a great deal of touch and bellowing in my ear so that I could make out what she was saying. By the end of two weeks she was very hoarse but amazingly, did not lose her patience at any point with me – only realising that I was totally up against it. When the hospital gave me the all-clear eleven weeks later, I celebrated by going to hear the pianist Stephen Hough give a recital at Saffron Hall. I had the privilege of meeting him after the concert and I told him about my recent enforced imprisonment by deafness – he, like me, was very emotional. He played a wonderful rendition of Schubert's Ave Maria which was very prayerful in its way. I was able to hear every single note and I have never thanked God so much for being able to hear that day and subsequent days thanks to wonderful hearing aids that put the range of sound back for me. Whenever there are situations like this where you have to go through difficult times with your carer, it is a very emotionally-binding experience and obviously very challenging, yet I hope this is when the carer feels that the job is then worthwhile. It is not just about the toileting and feeding question but the humanity of the job, in fact, it is more than a job – it is, and should be, a vocation, especially if you believe in what you are doing it for. Those people who deal with end of life care, supporting families and giving the person they are caring for a quality of life until life's end, have my complete and utter admiration because when palliative care is given a carer may only have a very short time – days or weeks, to get to know and steer the family through so much emotion. I don't know whether I would ever be in the position to deal with such circumstances. Hospices, where the doctors, nurses, and carers are so involved, do a wonderful job with their complete and utter dedication.

I have spoken about some of the carers who regularly supported me and I became very fond of them. Pat, was also one such person. She went on to train as a nurse, something that I know that she always wanted to do. I wish her all the luck in the world.

However, there is one person who stands out for special mention due to her kindness and dedication – that is Mary Ann. I knew that we would get on from the very moment we met – she is exceedingly gentle, kind and considerate. She doesn't assume without asking and takes my requests and needs into full consideration. It is certainly not a 'them' and 'us' situation but a partnership which for good care to work, is essential. Her attention to detail is amazing – the small things really matter to her and me for example, warming my clothes before they are put on, and warming the very cold sling before she puts it on my back in the morning, especially in the winter. She is funny and has a wonderful sense of humour along with good old Irish wit. At the start of the Coronavirus pandemic Mary Ann and I were thrust together – she had come over from Spain (where she lives) for my 70th Birthday Party which was on the 18th March 2020 then the Coronavirus 'lockdown' announcement came into force on the 23rd March. Sadly, my special Birthday had to be cancelled but Mary Ann tried to make it as special as she could by cooking a beautiful meal and giving me flowers and chocolates etc. One of Mary Ann's great assets is that she comes from a background in catering – her family owned a restaurant in Southern Ireland for many years so she can turn her hand to almost anything. I have been totally spoilt and I appreciate her beautiful cooking skills - as a blind person, taste, smell, and texture is vitally important. Mary Ann has learnt the things that I like and I have tried many new dishes under her expert hand. During lockdown we have occupied ourselves by reading some 20 books on 'Audible' and Mary Ann has read many articles of interest and keeps me up to date on what she finds on her mobile phone which of course, is a great source of reference. I want to make it quite clear that for Mary Ann to spend 17 weeks caring for me was a great feat of human endeavour, even though she did have some relief from Melody. We have spent many happy hours sitting in the garden chatting and sharing music and books together. I will always appreciate her help and want to thank her publicly for everything that she has done.

When Two Worlds Collide

For this chapter I want to highlight issues relating to the cost of care and the ramifications of it. We currently live in a society where those who need care are in an unenviable position. If one has been frugal and put money by for a rainy day and tried to have a culture of savings, then one quickly realises that if you or the person you care for is in need of professional care support, life becomes extremely difficult. If you have more than the allowance allotted by social services of £23,225 then anything over that figure if a person requires care, is all down to the person paying for themselves. This, to me, seems totally archaic and this so-called needs-led service is a total nonsense. Someone needing care does not have a needs-led service. That would imply that social services would meet the requirements of the individual but sadly that is not the case. What you quickly realise is that if you are going to need long term care in the future then it is not in your interest to have savings in a bank or building society. Sadly, there is no way of hiding your cash because the local authority will check on any bank account and you are not allowed to give your personal funds away to make it look as though you do not have money. Any attempt to do so would be regarded as fraudulent and you will be told to recoup that money. The local authority is not interested in any excuse that you try to make. It seems to me that the only way that you can ease your financial burden is to put your money into a personal possession such as a picture, jewellery, fine wines or any other legal loophole to shed your money. It seems terrible that people have to resort to such tactics especially when you have built up a nest egg of personal funds which is then whittled away by the need to pay for care. So far, I have spent £376,000, which is still rising every month, in care costs of my own money – well over the cost of an average home. Perhaps there will be those thinking why bother? Why not use your money. Have what you want throughout your life and disregard the consequences. Now that I have had to pay virtually all of my money in this way I have some sympathy with that view but I also realise that the local authorities/government do not have a bottomless pocket. However, having made such an effort and virtually lost everything, paying what I was meant to pay, then I feel that this is a gross infringement of my own personal finance and personal dignity. There are so many things that I require. A wheelchair that is absolutely suitable for my needs – you would perhaps feel that this is my fundamental right but rights don't seem to come into it. It is hard when others have so much and now I have virtually nothing. I would love the luxury of £23,225 in my bank account but at the moment as I write this I am overdrawn on almost every account, robbing Peter to pay Paul every week to try to make ends meet and by and large I am not succeeding. The world has gone mad when some have so much and others so little and sadly very few help you to get out of a mess. Up until now I have been able to work on a regular basis since 1970 and I have supported myself fully. I must say that I have felt immensely proud that despite multiple disability, I have achieved this - running a house, paying a mortgage, running a car, and meeting all my general living expenses for myself and a twenty-four-hour carer. However, the emotional cost of juggling so many balls in the air and having to fight with social services for aids and adaptations is truly a nightmare. I know that my situation is not unique. There are thousands of people up and down the country (more than a quarter of a million profoundly disabled people alone) that find themselves in this disastrous situation. Let us take an example of someone who is a business man with a highly paid job, a wife, and family. Overnight, his life changes within the blinking of an eye – he suffers a stroke, which affects his speech, his mobility, his bodily functions and of course his financial situation. It is hard enough for a family to cope with these new-found circumstances from an emotional point of view but put everything else into the mix with the family, then the pressure on other members of the family, and in particular the existing partner, is crucifying. Most people do not know which way to turn. There is normally quite a feeling of panic. One does not know where to start. Firstly, one has to see whether there is going to be any level of improvement on the part of the person who has had the stroke, the consequences of which maybe catastrophic, causing them to have difficulty with swallowing, eating, and of course bowel and bladder functionality. The immediate response from hospital and social services is the issue of limited resources. The normal provision is two bed sheets and two pads in any one day. It is a harsh reality that people's toilet function is not restricted to twice a day! The reality is probably around eight times a day (depending on the level that the person drinks, and overnight the financial burden is exhausting, causing the family to pay more than £100 a month in pads, sheets, masks, aprons etc. If one wants to keep scrupulously clean it has to be worked at so there is an almost inexhaustible supply of wet wipes and/or dry wipes and the like, to aid the cleaning process. All the while the individual or carer is seeing their finances being soaked-up like through a straw in a bottle of coke and you are left wondering how the hell you are going to cope. What's more, very few people care about how you will cope and this is why so many people have an undesirable odour of incontinence about their person. Not only does the person who has become disabled have to suffer all the indignities but they also have to give chapter and verse on every aspect of their care. A great many hate the process so much that they would rather suffer than share their personal needs with a group of people from social services. There is a game that is played by social services which is, 'We recognize your needs and those of your carer, but it is par for the course to put the carer on their knees before help can be given.' This is where Britain falls down and at the end no one really wins. What carers and patients experience are rounds of endless scrutiny into every aspect of their lives that once was private and now has become an open door of public scrutiny. There is no sense of privacy and one's life becomes an open book for all to pore over. It is something I absolutely hate because I feel it is so unjust. When so much personal finance has been eroded and the carer is almost having to be hospitalised because they are so exhausted, then they decide to bring in care agencies 'to help.' Thereby hangs a tale – care agencies are stretched beyond measure to provide a dignified level of care for the patient but at what price? If the patient requires a live-in carer 24/7 then we know that the problems are going to be enormous – often, a new carer every week, which doesn't help with continuity nor trying to build a good working relationship. Tempers can often get frayed and the client is left, wanting to pull their hair out in frustration. Of course, this is not a one-way ticket. I am sure carers feel exactly the same while they are with certain clients. The saddest part of all this is that carers do everything that they can (hopefully) to make the person as comfortable as possible but their needs are grossly under estimated and under funded for what they do. No other person working in industry would have to be told that their shift is from 7 in the morning until 7 at night with two hours break but after 7pm if help is required you still have to give it and you will be paid a flat rate of between £25 and £29 for staying on the premises all night, being on-call when required. No one in their right mind would accept working conditions like these. Can you imagine if we told our company boss that they have to remain on shift for such a meagre wage and that they would not be allowed to leave the premises? I am sure that they would be up in arms, telling us what we could do with our care work!

To Pee or not to Pee?

When someone invites you out socially, you do not have to think twice about your response – it's either that you accept to go or you don't. When there is disability in the equation, it's a whole new ballgame. I frequently make trips to London to go to classical music venues such as The Barbican, Royal Festival Hall, Wigmore Hall, Royal Albert Hall and The Cadogan Hall and so on. I know that I am extremely lucky to have live-in carers or friends who will take me to such places because they know that I absolutely adore classical music – indeed, I would go so far as to say that classical music is my life. One of the worst nightmares is, needing to go to the toilet and not being able to execute that need. With the Radar key system, the situation for people with disabilities has dramatically improved but for the most part, many public toilets for the disabled are still very inadequate – being too small and without a hoist or closomat toilet. For the most part space is at a premium and often the water is cold and sinks are either extremely low or impracticably high with hand driers and paper towel dispensers awkwardly placed. Nevertheless we 'should be grateful.' So often, an evening is ruined because toilet facilities for people with disabilities are at best inadequate, and at worse, non-existent. It shouldn't all be about a suitable toilet for life is much more than being able to go to the loo. But sadly, by and large, a shopping expedition can mean just that. Shop assistants are often vague in attitude, completely ignoring the needs of the person with disability while they chat to their friends about what they did on the evening before. Often, there is little or no guidance to assist the person with disability and leaving someone with a sense that they have received good service is a rare commodity. If we want to feel completely integrated then perhaps we should look more to the Swedish and Helsinki models of social care where housing has to be accessible to all whether disabled or not. In Sweden, modern properties have to have wide doorways and be wheelchair-accessible because the Swedish government say that a person with disability should not be prevented from socialising with their able-bodied counterparts. What a revelation! In Britain most homes are not wheelchair-accessible because the doorways are not more than 26 inches wide. There are certainly no guards are on the doors to prevent scratching the paintwork etc. What saddens me about all of this is that for the most part, people do not invite a person with disabilities to their home because it is too problematic. Normally there is a very small toilet or even worse, the bathroom is upstairs. So, one has to spend much of the evening restricting liquid intake which is generally very bad for one's health. On hot summer days we need to drink as much as the next person but we find ourselves restricting our intake for fear of being a nuisance. We, sadly, have adopted the attitude of paying lip-service to the genuine needs of people with disability. The mood is changing but it is still woefully inadequate. There is a new breed of disability toilets called 'Changing Places.' There is a table that a disabled person can be hoisted onto and a closomat toilet that will wash and dry the person which is a vast improvement on what went on before. However, the tables are so narrow that you cannot turn your body adequately because there is often only access on one side of the table which is usually placed against a wall. This is self-defeating, of course, if clothing has to be readjusted. Perhaps the most difficult scenario is that these toilets are often closed late afternoon or sometimes before 10pm which presupposes that someone is not going to need a toilet after say 4pm therefore, if a changing places toilet is required, the brilliant idea is scuppered due to the fact that people are putting time restraints on our toilet needs. Whilst Changing Places is a brilliant idea they are very few and far between. There was one incident where, on presenting ourselves at The Victoria Embankment Gardens Changing Places Toilet, we read a notice pinned to the outside of the door which informed us that the toilet was out of order and that Westminster City Council are aware of this and are doing all that they can to rectify the situation. On subsequent trips to London, each time we passed the area the notice was still plastered on the door, indeed, this remained for more than six months. This is a truly disgusting state of affairs for if I said to all the able-bodied commuters travelling into London that they were not able to use the toilet facilities in London then I'm sure that the whole community would be in uproar. But don't worry about the consequences – it's only the disabled!

It's not just the disability toilet issue that has to be broken down. It's more about the attitude of the able-bodied. Two friends of mine, my husband, and myself booked to go to a restaurant. I was told that we had to get there early because the restaurant would be full so we booked our table for 6.30 in the evening. On a table for four I was placed facing a brick wall away from other patrons. When it came to ordering my meal the proprietor said to my friends in reference to myself, 'What does *she* want to eat?' I gave my answers clearly and distinctly but was ignored. This went on all through the meal. I felt more and more angry at the absolute ignorance of this man. When the coffees were brought I asked him what brandies he had. His response was '*You* drink brandy? Well what *brandies* do *you* like then?'

I said 'Hennesy Paradise Extra is quite good.'

His patronising response was '*You* drink *Hennesy Paradise Extra*!!!"

I responded 'Yes, it's rather good, isn't it?'

He walked away in utter bewilderment and disgust because I had had the temerity to want something that was, in his eyes, classy. I wasn't going to tell him that I had only drunk that wonderful brandy three times in my life before. I felt people like him deserve to be taught a lesson. My friends were disgusted by his attitude and response and they vowed that they would never frequent his restaurant again. Whilst I waited for the bill to be paid and my car to be brought nearer to the establishment, I was placed at the counter. I said to the man in question, 'You are lucky that I haven't brought a case of disability discrimination against you.'

He said that I did not know what I was talking about. I pointed out the way I was told to get there early as the restaurant would be full even though it was almost empty, left facing a blank wall, and ignored over the menu choices – none of which left me with a feeling of being wanted or respected. After all, my money is as good as anyone else's. So, he was left in no doubt as to our feelings.

Some months later, I attended a dinner of the Suffolk Dining Society. There were close on a hundred guests. I took a guest and a carer. The guest sat next to me on my left, the carer opposite. The person sitting next to me on my right was a professor of human biology. It was thought that I would find him interesting to talk to (nothing could be further from the truth). Our starter course arrived and was duly eaten and whilst they were using the brush to take the crumbs off the table, the professor turned to me and said, 'What you *need*, is one of those bibs that they use for a baby that has a gully at the bottom of it, then we could turn it upside down and see how much you have spilt!' My friend sitting on my left who just happened to be a doctor of medicine, leant over and said to him, 'Oh, you are a very brave man!'

My response to the professor was, 'Anymore remarks like that and you will get my dinner straight over your head!'

'Oh, that's not very nice,' he said.

I retorted 'Why did you think it was necessary to say such a thing?'

His answer was, 'Because I thought you could take it.'

I explained, 'Actually, I can't take it. I find situations like this one, very difficult – always worrying whether I will spill something and how I will manage. I come here once a month to meet people and have some interesting conversation and enjoyment and now you have spoilt it by your comments.'

Nothing more was said until the dessert was completed and the coffee arrived – more brushing of the table ensued. The professor turned to me and said, 'I have made much more mess than you.' To which I completely ignored him. He then said, 'Why do you think that is?' I said, 'Years of practice, old son!' I also felt absolutely distraught that I had been put through such a difficult situation. Needless to say, I made it known to my friend and carer that I wished to leave as quickly as possible. I don't know why people find it necessary to comment in such a way. What should have happened is that they ask whether I perhaps needed any assistance and offered to help but the professor was so 'puffed-up' with his own importance that he forgot social graces, indeed, I don't think he had any.

Coronavirus Lockdown and its Frustrations

As I have already stated, Mary Ann was truly magnificent in helping me. On that evening of the 11th March, I had attended the Royal Festival Hall with my friend, Debbie, who was also my massage therapist. We both have a great love of music - Debbie sings in a choir and loves going to concerts when she is able but more importantly, we have a great respect for one another and a real genuine friendship. Little did I know when I arrived home late that evening that this was going to be my last musical occasion for around five months and that it would be ongoing. I know that there is much to be enjoyed from the playing of CD's but, in my opinion, there is nothing like a live concert. I have been given Christmas money by certain friends who know how much I love music so that I can enjoy specialist concerts so I save up any spare cash or Christmas money to buy a wheelchair and escort ticket for many concert venues in London, Suffolk, Essex and anywhere else it happens to be. I always love to experience new places or go further afield when circumstances will allow but for now,

at this point in time, all I had during lockdown was the frustration and feeling of being totally stuck, unlike my able-bodied counterparts, who were able to go to the shops when necessary. My carer was given notification that as a key-worker she would be able to go to Waitrose store from 7 until 8 in the morning whereupon I was left in bed so that she could complete this task without any impedance from me. Fortunately, at 7 in the morning, I was quite happy to curl up in bed and leave someone else to complete that task.

It has often been quite difficult to find a suitable slot for online shopping – most supermarkets made so-called provision for carers so that they could get back to the people that they were looking after but I don't think that this went far enough. Often we were booking an online slot for three weeks ahead otherwise it would not have been available. Meanwhile, I am largely stuck just sitting on my patio and in my garden soaking up the sunshine and vitamin D. The only time that I had left my home was to go out in my car, although when my carers went to a shop, I hadn't been able to go with them into the actual shop. It was frustrating and seemingly pointless as I was not able to see the scenery or even watch the people go by – all I ended up with was a sore bottom as I got bumped over many holes in the road. One doesn't realise how important it is for the wellbeing of others to have good maintenance of the infrastructure such as roads and pavements. It is also difficult, even when one is allowed, to sit outside in a beer garden when one doesn't know the heights of tables and one is faced with social distancing, which wouldn't be easy moving someone in a wheelchair if barriers are put in place. I spent most of my time de-sprigging thousands of blackcurrants – these were bought in local farm shops and supermarkets and some from my own bushes which were newly-purchased last year. Thanks to Amazon I was able to purchase the multipurpose compost and other goodies that I needed including the large pots (4 in all). Bags of compost are extremely heavy for some people to lift so even tackling a small task such as the planting of blackcurrant bushes costs a lot and it is often very inconvenient when carers are busy doing other things like caring for me and we have to stop ordering.

The one thing that kept me sane, apart from the de-sprigging of the blackcurrants, were the telephone calls made and received between myself and others. In the latter days of lockdown I had been able to see people in my garden and, joy of joys, get a haircut. I didn't appreciate how marvellous this would feel – to know that you are somehow back in the world and not giving up. I have also spent time clearing much clutter from my office – hundreds of sheets of paper from years back. Even though this task was problematic, due to not being able to see text myself, it got done and my shredding machine worked overtime.

The one thing that I have found the hardest to bear is that neighbours next door to me never even passed the time of day or asked if my carer needed any assistance. It was assumed that we were alright Jack but every task that had to be completed outside the home, took so much longer because of the virus. People on the streets were inevitably far too busy to even have a distant conversation. No one seemed to offer any time to help my carers. It would have been so incredibly helpful if people had offered to check up that we were ok and ask whether they could add anything to their shopping bill for me.

One aspect of the Coronavirus which has been extremely difficult, is the conflicting messages issued by the Government. With hindsight we can say that it was wrong for the Government not to enforce lock-down much earlier than March 23rd. But, as they say, hindsight is a wonderful thing – we can all be bold after the event. I feel that, not to have sufficient mask and PPE equipment in the early days of lockdown, was quite frankly, a disgrace. Care homes and other medical organizations such as GP's, Dentists, and Chiropodists should have always had protective equipment available rather than scrabbling around urgently looking for supplies. I know that many people thought that the social distancing rules were a little over the top but this wretched virus keeps on coming. Now we don't know where we are. The consequences for visually-impaired people are extremely challenging. If one has to use a long cane or 'white Stick' it can be very difficult for the visually-impaired to establish where they are with limited vision. I have heard of one particular incident concerning a lady who was deaf/blind trying to communicate with her carer who was reading some information to her. To do this she had to partially remove her mask so that she could communicate with the deaf/blind person much to the annoyance of other people on the train who could not understand the problem. Other passengers became abusive to the blind person which was quite unforgiveable — especially when the carer explained what the problem was.

In the past, passers-by would offer assistance to the visually-impaired person when crossing a road or dealing with a busy junction. Now many blind/partially-sighted people are left floundering because what little vision they may have has caused confusion due to the fact that they have to wear a mask and try to cope. Many Blind lobbyists made representation about this problem to the Government. Then the Government edict was that blind people did not have to wear a mask but the abuse from the Public still keeps coming with little or no perception as to the problems. For me, one of my biggest problems, has been the institutionalislim of being stuck in my garden.

Once lock-down restrictions started to be eased, I was taken for a ride to a Thai Restaurant and latterly an outdoor 'al fresco' folk music and pizza evening at Snape Maltings concert gardens on the Hepworth Lawn. This was pleasant, but for me, nothing beats an indoor concert with an orchestra.

Overall, we had been saturated by Covid information and figures that were mind-blowing to the point of ad nauseam and one wondered when or if it would ever end? The answer, in part, was of course, the vaccine. In the past, I have bad reactions to FLU jabs so I have now given up on them and have managed very well so far, but this Covid virus was a whole new ball game. I not only had to think of my own health needs but also those of my carers. What I'd like more than anything else is for life to have a sense of normality rather than utter bewilderment and confusion. Thankfully, the ability to attend live concerts has been reinstated.

Conclusion

Up until now we have incidents that do not throw a very good light on the carer-client relationship, but here is a little story that will dispel the feelings of inadequacy which in my mind are very prevalent with care work. This particular Sunday when we had just come back from church, there was suddenly a very loud clicking noise and all the electric trips went off. I asked my carer to go to the hall cupboard. She could not find the door as it was completely dark and she could not even find her way out of the bedroom, through the kitchen and into the hallway. She was completely rooted to the spot, so I did what was fundamental to all blind people by asking her to follow the sound of my voice.
'But I can't see,' was her response.
'But you don't have to see,' I replied, 'Just follow my voice.' I proceeded to make my way into the hallway and, after a great deal of talking and trying to build her confidence, she eventually found the door of the hall cupboard. I told her to open the door and put her hand forward until she found a polythene bag hanging up in which there were candles and matches and a couple of small dishes in which to put the candles. She was completely stuck, and in the end I told her to stand back and I would find the candles, which I duly did. I put the candles into the dishes, struck the match which gave my carer a degree of light, and passed the match on to her to light the candle. She was incredulous that I had managed to do this without seeing. I laughed and said, 'But I have a power cut every single day.' Her response was 'Yes but it's not pitch black for you is it?' 'Of course it is! I don't have any eyes in my head!' I replied. She could still not get her head around the fact that every day was dark for me. The next day, I went and bought a rechargeable hurricane lamp which carers keep by the bed for emergencies. It's something that my carer and I have laughed about very often, however there is a serious side to all of this, which is, that unless they truly experience the

difficulties, they have no real concept of what I face on a daily basis, which to me is incredible. It's not rocket science.

I had one carer who saw me with my artificial eyes out one day, and his reaction was 'now I can really believe that you are blind'. I know that the prosthetic artist who painted my prosthesis did a wonderful job; most people would never know that I wasn't sighted. This can work against me sometimes, but the fact that I wish to be as 'normal' as possible is very important to me. As I have stated, there weren't many times when my carers were victorious on my behalf; I had been preparing for the publication of my third book, but as we came up to launch day, I knew that due to illness, (I was suffering from vitamin D deficiency), I would not be able to attend, so with great reluctance I prepared a speech as to why I would not be able to make it, making the appropriate apologies. Unbeknownst to me, my carers had spoken to two of my friends about the possibilities of being helped into my outdoor wheelchair so that I could attend. My carer came in to see me that morning and I was very upset about not being able to go. She said 'I am going to prepare you for going.' But I still insisted that I would not be able to make it and was very anxious. She insisted on getting me washed and dressed for the event. Later that morning, two of my friends suddenly arrived; they physically picked me up and put me in my wheelchair. 'I'm going, I'm going' I exclaimed. I couldn't actually believe that I had made it this far. Suddenly I found myself in the back of my vehicle. I felt a little disorientated, yet absolutely elated. I telephoned my agent and said to her that I was on my way, travelling to the University of Suffolk for the event. As soon as I arrived, there was a great deal of activity. People had heard the rumour that I was going to make it despite my illness. When I arrived people were cheering and applauding that I had actually made it. There was much excitement with photographers, journalists and media people milling around.

At the event I was able to express my joy at the fact that I had actually made it and gave a speech that was as professional as ever.

How pleased I was, and how proud that my two carers for the day were so delighted, they have always said it was a day they would never forget. It was certainly one of the high spots and it just goes to show how people with disability can fully engage in the world around them, and take their place as an equal human being. However, that engagement into the world can only occur if there are carers who are willing to enable this to happen. I am so fortunate now, that I have a male carer who shares the same love of classical music as I do. He has a degree in music history and is a player of brass instruments. Whilst that is his first love, he greatly enjoys all types of music. We have much fun and companionship, talking about and sharing music together. My life has been transformed from a person who hardly went outside the door, to a person who goes regularly to concerts in London, so much so that these concerts have been almost weekly for the last five months. Long may they continue!

One carer has made such a difference. I would not have dreamed it possible that I have got my old lifestyle back, of regular concert going, and that is wonderful. What it proves is that one person can either make or break the caring relationship. If all things were equal in this life, it should not be possible for one person to make such a difference. If the job is done well, then the role of the carer should be to enhance the client's life, but sadly I have learnt to my cost that this kind of situation rarely happens.

I have written about those incidents that have stayed firmly in my mind over these last ten years, which proves how tough it can be to try and hold your life together, especially when all forces seem to be working against you. However, there are many more that I have not quoted here, or indeed I have let slip through the net. What needs to happen is that carers must have a genuine desire to create change, for this is much more than 'just a job' and our whole purpose for change is to improve the lives of those that we care for, and if there is not a genuine desire for that change, then go and do something less emotionally demanding.

All people have a desire for their lives to improve. Let's work for that to happen.

'On a Count of Three' by Dr Lin Berwick MBE MCIOJ ©

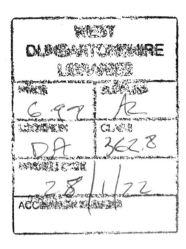
Printed in Great Britain
by Amazon

75702846R00038